CONSTITUTIONAL CONVENTION (PHILADELPHIA, 1787)

A. LAWYERS, MERCHANTS, AND PLANTERS

1. **Prominent** members included J. Madison, A. Hamilton, J. Dickinson, B. Franklin, and G. Morris.
2. **G. Washington** elected as presiding officer.
3. J. Madison's Virginia Plan called for bicameral legislature with representation based on population and an executive branch.
4. W. Paterson's New Jersey Plan, defeated in mid-June, called for increased power for national government while maintaining a unicameral Congress with equal representation for states.
5. Impasse resolved by introduction of R. Sherman's **Connecticut (Great) Compromise** calling for a **bicameral legislature** with a Senate with equal representation and a House of Representatives with representation based on population, as well as an executive branch.
6. **Three-Fifths Compromise** called for three of every five slaves to be counted for determining both population and taxation for states.
7. **President** and vice president to be chosen by an **electoral college**.
8. **President** to have the power to veto legislation and **conduct foreign policy**.
9. **Congress** to have the power to impeach and remove president.
10. **New Constitution** to take effect when nine of the 13 states had approved.

B. RATIFICATION OF THE CONSTITUTION

1. **Federalists** argued for passage in *The Federalist Papers* authored by J. Madison, A. Hamilton, and J. Jay.
2. **Anti-Federalists** opposed the new government.
3. In June 1788 the Constitution was ratified by nine states.
4. **Virginia** held out until framers promised a bill of rights.
5. **North Carolina** finally ratified in November 1788 and Rhode Island held out until May 1790.
6. **Washington** was inaugurated as first president in March 1789, and the first Congress convened in New York City.

THE FEDERALIST ERA (1789-1800)

A. GEORGE WASHINGTON AND JOHN ADAMS –
elected in 1789 and again in 1792, with predominantly Federalist Congress.

1. **Judiciary Act** of 1789 created Supreme Court and **system of district and appeals courts**.
2. **Executive departments** created—state, treasury, war, attorney-general—became nucleus of cabinet.
3. **Bill of Rights**, the first 10 amendments to the Constitution, adopted in 1791.

B. TREASURY SECRETARY HAMILTON – presented
his "Report on Manufacturers" and "Report on the Public Credit," outlining program to build a strong central government and an economy based on industry and commerce. Jefferson opposed this program.

C. EMERGENCE OF POLITICAL PARTIES

1. The pro-Hamilton **Federalists** favored strong central government, "loose" interpretation of Constitution, and encouragement of business and urbanism.
2. Jefferson and Madison's **Republicans** wanted small government, "strict" interpretation, and development of an agrarian, rural society.

D. FOREIGN AFFAIRS

1. **French Revolutionary** Wars (1792) prompted a **Proclamation of Neutrality**, but U.S. actually traded with both sides.
2. **Jay Treaty** (1794) with Britain settled few issues, but bought time for U.S.
3. **Pinckney Treaty** (1795) with Spain opened the Mississippi River to American traffic and settled the northern boundary of Florida.

E. BATTLE OF FALLEN TIMBERS (1794) – General
Anthony Wayne defeated the British-backed Indians and cleared the Ohio territory.

F. WHISKEY REBELLION (1794) – Federal response
in crushing the protest to the new whiskey tax strengthened credibility of the new federal government.

G. ELECTION OF 1796 – Adams and Jefferson elected.
Split ticket produced conflict-ridden administration.

1. **XYZ Affair** – French tried to bribe American diplomats. Anti-French sentiment surged at home.
2. **Quasi war with France (1798-1799)** – Department of the Navy created to defend American shipping.
3. **Alien and Sedition Acts** promoted by Adams to suppress dissent and the growing power of Republican opposition.
4. **Kentucky and Virginia Resolutions (1798, 1799)** – Jefferson and Madison protested the Alien and Sedition Acts by proposing a process of nullification of unpopular laws by injured states.

THE JEFFERSONIAN ERA (1801-1825)

A. THE REVOLUTION OF 1800 – saw Jefferson
elected president by the House, after electoral confusion with vice-presidential nominee Aaron Burr.

1. Conflict with the courts – Adams' Judiciary Act of 1801 packed the court system with last-minute Federalist appointees.
   a. *Marbury v. Madison* – Marshall's court failed to seat Adams' appointee, and thus asserted the doctrine of judicial review.

B. LOUISIANA PURCHASE (1803)

1. Napoleon's ambitions for a New World Empire died in Santo Domingo, and he was ready to sell.
2. Jefferson violated his own "strict interpretation" stand and paid less than three cents per acre, doubling U.S. territory.
3. Lewis and Clark were soon mapping the new lands (1804-1806); Zebulon Pike and others were also exploring the West.

C. THE BURR CONSPIRACY

1. Aaron Burr killed Hamilton in a duel. Burr became involved in a scheme to seize Texas from Mexico. Charged with treason in 1806.
2. Burr was acquitted, frustrating Jefferson's demands for "executive privilege" and helping to establish the guidelines for treason prosecutions.

D. FOREIGN RELATIONS

1. Barbary Wars ended in a stalemate.
2. Napoleonic Wars drew America into the conflict because U.S. tried to trade with both sides.
3. Chesapeake-Leopard Affair (1807) involved British violation of U.S. neutrality at sea.
4. Embargo of 1807 was Jefferson's attempt to stay out of war by shutting off all trade with Europe. Economic disaster.

E. MADISON'S ADMINISTRATION (1809-1817)

1. Indian problems on the frontier were exploited by British.
2. War Hawks persuaded Madison to ask Congress for war declaration in 1812.
3. In the North, U.S. invasion of Canada failed. The Battle of Lake Erie in 1813 was an American victory, as was the Battle of the Thames in Canada.
4. Battle of Horseshoe Bend (Alabama, 1814) thrust Andrew Jackson into the public eye.

5. British invasion of Chesapeake Bay was stopped at Fort McHenry, Baltimore, after Washington, D.C. was burned.
6. At New Orleans, January 1815, Jackson defeated the British, two weeks after the Treaty of Ghent was signed, restoring the prewar political status quo.
7. **Hartford Convention (1814)** – New England Federalists met and threatened secession if their commercial interests were not protected. This discredited the Federalists.

F. MONROE'S ADMINISTRATION (1817-1825)

1. Known as the "Era of Good Feelings."
2. **Rush-Bagot Treaty (1817)** – A disarmament agreement to demilitarize the Great Lakes.
3. **Adams-Onis Treaty (1819)** – Spain sold Florida to the U.S.
4. **Monroe Doctrine (1823)** – Declared that the Western Hemisphere was off-limits to European colonization.

INTERNAL DEVELOPMENT – POST-WAR OF 1812

A. THE MARSHALL COURT

1. Chief Justice John Marshall built the power of the central government and the Court.
   a. *Marbury v. Madison* (1803) – Established the right of the Court to rule on constitutionality of federal laws.
   b. *Fletcher v. Peck* (1810) – Court declared a state law constitutional.
   c. *Dartmouth College* (1819) – Upheld the sanctity of contracts against state action.
   d. *McCulloch v. Maryland* (1819) – Established federal immunity from states' taxing power.
   e. *Gibbons v. Ogden* (1824) – Established federal control over interstate commerce.

B. THE MISSOURI COMPROMISE (1820)

1. Missouri's application for statehood raised the issue of slavery's extension into the territories.
2. Henry Clay's compromise admitted Missouri as a slave state, balanced with free Maine, but drew a line to the Pacific Coast, limiting the extension of slavery.

C. THE ECONOMY

1. The Northeast, the South, and the new West were all booming, but on different tracks of development.
2. Immigration increased, as well as migration to the West, which mostly consisted of small farms.
3. The Cotton Kingdom was expanding into the new Gulf states.
4. Roads and canals were expanding, creating a national market.
5. Unions developed, but very slowly.

D. EDUCATION

1. Public schools were slow to deve[lop] schools were private and expensive.
2. Higher education was limited [and] usually church-related, male-dominate[d]. Professional schools were scarce.
3. Noah Webster's speller and [ ] ned the basis for literacy.
4. Washington Irving, Mercy Otis [ ] and "Parson" Weems were well-known [ ]

E. RELIGION

1. The Second Great Awakening [ ]nse to the secular influence of the Enli[ghtenment] and the Scientific Revolution. Revival[ ]he South and swept across the nation, [ ] spark the movement for reform.
2. Peter Cartwright was a prominent preacher in this movement.

JACKSONIAN DEMOCRACY (1829-1841)

A. ELECTION OF 1824 – went to the House, even though Andrew Jackson won the popular vote. John Quincy Adams won the election, and Jackson vowed revenge, claiming a "corrupt bargain" with Henry Clay. **The Tariff of Abominations** (1828), which imposed high import duties, was bitterly denounced by the South.

B. ELECTION OF 1828
1. Jackson elected handily on the Democratic ticket after a dirty campaign on both sides.
2. Jackson perceived as a "man of the people," promoted the spoils system and exercised his veto freely.

C. INDIAN REMOVAL ACT (1830) – provided for the removal of all Indian tribes to lands west of the Mississippi River. Many tribes resisted, with the **Cherokee Trail of Tears** one result.

D. NULLIFICATION THREAT – John C. Calhoun resigned the vice presidency and drew up an **Ordinance of Nullification**, proposing a process by which a state could ignore a federal law it found distasteful. Jackson's response was the **Force Bill**, by which he threatened to enforce the tariff with the army. Calhoun backed down.

E. THE BANK WAR – Jackson distrusted the U.S. Bank and vetoed its charter renewal. He then removed the government deposits and put them into his "pet banks," precipitating a recession. In 1836 his Specie Circular plunged the country into a long-term depression.

F. THE ELECTION OF 1836 – saw Martin van Buren, Jackson's choice, take the presidency.

G. THE ELECTION OF 1840 – saw the first Whig president, William Henry Harrison, win with a "log cabin" appeal to the common man. He died within a month, and John Tyler took over.

H. JACKSONIAN POLITICS
1. The beginnings of the modern party system, with its organization, platform, and conventions.
2. The strong executive dominated his party.
3. New emphasis on states' rights – *Charles River Bridge* case (1837) – Returned the commerce power to the states, when in the public interest.
4. The rise of the Whigs, with their support of commercial and industrial development, led by Clay, Calhoun, and Daniel Webster.

ANTE-BELLUM CULTURE

A. THE REFORM IMPULSE
1. Sources were in European Romanticism and in the desire for control over the changing social scene.
2. Centered in New England

B. EXAMPLES OF THE MOVEMENT
1. Literature
   a. Northern writers: James F. Cooper, Walt Whitman, Henry W. Longfellow, Herman Melville, Francis Parkman, Nathaniel Hawthorne
   b. Southern writers: Edgar Allan Poe, William Gilmore Simms
2. Fine Arts
   a. Painters: Hudson River School, George Catlin's Indians, John J. Audubon's birds
   b. Theater and minstrel shows
3. Transcendentalists tried to gain unity with God outside organized religion – Ralph Waldo Emerson, Henry David Thoreau.
4. Utopians tried to escape the industrial world by retreating to communal life.
   a. Secular communities: Brook Farm (Mass.), New Harmony (Indiana), Nashoba (Tenn.), Amana (Iowa)
   b. Religious communities: The Shakers, The Mormons (Joseph Smith and Brigham Young)

C. POLITICAL REFORM MOVEMENTS
1. Temperance movement began in 1826; had strong anti-Catholic overtones.
2. Public schools were scattered, Protestant-oriented, and mostly Northern. There was much early opposition. Horace Mann in Massachusetts was early advocate; Henry Barnard in Connecticut.
3. Feminism had origins in the Seneca Falls Convention, 1848, and was linked with the abolitionists (Elizabeth Cady Stanton).
4. Abolitionism originated with William Lloyd Garrison's "The Liberator" (1831) and his New England Anti-Slavery Society (1832).
   a. Theodore Weld, Frederick Douglass
   b. The Liberty Party fielded a presidential candidate in 1840.

D. EDUCATING THE PUBLIC
1. The age of oratory, patriotic holiday speeches.
2. Newspapers and magazines multiplied ("Godey's Ladies Book").
3. Colleges sprang up from religious roots or local "boosterism."
4. The Lyceum movement.

LIFE IN THE NORTH

A. POPULATION TRENDS
1. U.S. population grew from 4 million in 1790 to 32 million in 1860. The greatest increase was in the new West.
2. Birth rate decreased along with family size. "Cult of Domesticity" shifted family rearing to the woman.
3. Immigration increased after 1815, mostly from Britain, Germany, and Ireland.

B. URBAN GROWTH
1. Fivefold increase in urban population from 1790 to 1860.
2. Services and quality of life lagged. Social unrest and crime.
3. Anti-Catholic sentiments widespread.

C. MINORITIES
1. Women limited in economic and political participation. Sojourner Truth and Lucretia Mott traveled and spoke for women's rights.
2. Blacks were at the bottom of the ladder, threatened by immigrant labor and legal discrimination. African Methodist Episcopal Church flourished in cities.

D. INDUSTRY GREW RAPIDLY – The Northeast led the way, producing two-thirds of manufactured goods.
1. Technology was ahead of Europe – Eli Whitney's interchangeable parts, Elias Howe's sewing machine, Samuel B. Morse's telegraph.
2. Corporate form of ownership grew apace.
3. Labor began to organize, championed 10-hour day. Immigration spurred unions, but weakened their bargaining position.

E. AGRICULTURE – profitability rose as cities grew.
1. Technology was applied to farming, as in McCormick's reaper, John Deere's steel plow, and Case's thresher.

F. TRANSPORTATION – The railroad was assuming importance by 1840. Most lines ran east and west, tying the East to the new West.

G. DOMESTIC LIFE – was still primitive for the rural or urban working man. Wage-earners first exceeded the self-employed in 1860.

LIFE IN THE SOUTH

A. THE COTTON KINGDOM
1. Population and economic power shifted to the newly opened Gulf states, for cotton cultivation.
2. By 1850, 3 million bales annually were produced, for two-thirds of the value of U.S. exports.

B. CLASS SOCIETY
1. Planter class (50+ slaves) were the minority, but they dominated social and political life.
2. One-half of slave-owning families owned fewer than six slaves.
3. Yeoman farmers were the largest group, owned few

or no slaves. They raised corn, pigs, foodstuffs.
4. Poor whites ("crackers") formed an underclass.

C. THE SLAVE SYSTEM
1. Gang system used in lower South for staple crops. Hardest on the workers.
2. Task system used on smaller farms. Much less oppressive for the workers.
3. Domestic servants had it best, but more often were exploited personally.
4. Urban slaves often worked for wages, sometimes in industry. They were seen as threats to the stability of the system, so their numbers decreased.

D. THE SLAVE TRADE – Importation was illegal after 1808, but internal trade flourished. Movement was toward the new Gulf states from the old upper South.

E. THE RESPONSE OF SLAVES
1. Rebellions were fairly frequent. Gabriel Prosser (1800), Denmark Vesey (1822), and Nat Turner (1831) were best known.
2. Running away was a frequent solution, and many succeeded. Harriet Tubman helped 300 to escape.
3. "Soldiering," avoiding work, was the most popular form of resistance.
4. Black culture survived, family ties were strengthened in some cases, in the face of oppression.

F. COMMERCE AND INDUSTRY
1. The South developed an industrial base but lagged far behind the North.
2. Textiles, iron goods, and flour milling were profitable.
3. Most goods were consumed locally; little exported.
4. Commerce was limited to the needs of the planters. Factors served as merchants and bankers.
5. Some Southerners advocated change (DeBow's "Review") but were unheeded. The social system was built on the agrarian model, and cotton was profitable.

G. DOMESTIC LIFE
1. The plantation wife served a vital role in running the farms.
2. High birth and death rates.
3. Education was available only to the sons of the well-to-do. Few public schools.
4. Average living conditions inferior to the North. Dietary deficiencies common.

H. RESPONSE TO ANTI-SLAVERY MOVEMENT
1. Dissent was suppressed in the South.
2. After 1832, political discussion of emancipation ceased.
3. Southern congressmen imposed the "Gag Rule" in the U.S. House in 1836.
4. John C. Calhoun's theory of the "concurrent majority" tried to preserve Southern power.

MANIFEST DESTINY AND WESTWARD EXPANSION

A. LEWIS AND CLARK EXPEDITION – opened the new West to traders, trappers, and settlers.

B. THE OREGON COUNTRY – was jointly occupied by Britain and the U.S. by 1820. The Oregon Trail was carrying thousands west by the 1840s.

C. TEXAS – had welcomed American settlers since 1820, and by 1835 35,000 "gringos" were living there.
1. Texans declared independence from Mexico in 1836.
2. Santa Anna tried to put down rebellion.
3. After the loss of the Alamo, Sam Houston defeated Mexican army at San Jacinto, April 1836.
4. U.S. Congress refused to annex Texas because of the slavery issue, so Texans formed an independent nation.

D. CALIFORNIA – receiving increased American immigration.

E. THE SANTA FE TRAIL – was opening up American trade with the Southwest.

F. "MANIFEST DESTINY" – the belief that Americans should own land to the Pacific divided the nation further. Democrats favored the use of force to expand; the Whigs were more conservative. The question of whether slavery would "follow the flag" became increasingly divisive.